SUITES

FEDERICO GARCÍA LORCA

SUITES

*Translated from the Spanish
by Jerome Rothenberg*

GREEN INTEGER
KØBENHAVN & LOS ANGELES
2001

GREEN INTEGER
Edited by Per Bregne
København/Los Angeles

Distributed in the United States by Consortium Book
Sales and Distribution, 1045 Westgate Drive, Suite 90
Saint Paul, Minnesota 55114-1065

(323) 857-1115 / http://www.greeninteger.com

10 9 8 7 6 5 4 3 2 1

Design: Per Bregne
Typography: Guy Bennett
Photograph: Photograph of Federico García Lorca

LIBRARY OF CONGRESS CATALOGING IN PUBLICATION DATA
Lorca, Federico García [1898–1936]
Suites
ISBN: 1-892295-61-X
p. cm — Green Integer: 31
I. Title II. Series

Green Integer books are published for Douglas Messerli.

Printed in the United States of America on acid-free paper.

Contents

As a type of "serial poetry" (Robin Blaser's and Jack Spicer's term), the "suites" come early in Lorca's career but already show a connection with the montage & vernacular methods of early European modernism. Many remained unpublished during his lifetime & were later reassembled from notebooks in André Belamich's critical edition (1983). When I first attended to the several that had surfaced earlier, they struck me in large part as a different kind of Lorca than I had known before— still characteristically his but with a coolness & (sometimes) quirkiness, a playfulness of mind & music that I found instantly attractive. The full run of suites shows other Lorca characteristics as well, but my attempt, as far as I could, has been to stress these, as if to pay homage by so doing to this most graceful & elegant of twentieth-century poets. Toward those ends I have moved where needed between the literal & playful, but I have tried throughout to stay within Lorca's range & to avoid effects not clearly signaled by his own. (Here Christopher Maurer has acted as my trusted guide, & I thank him warmly for his efforts.) Federico García Lorca was one of the first poets to lead me & others of my generation into poetry, & his "wit and intelligence" (his "salt" in that Spanish idiom that turns up elsewhere in his work) have remained an inspiration to me across the decades.

Finally, I would like to dedicate these translations to the memory of Paul Blackburn—a poet, a friend, & a powerful translator of Lorca—who was there before me.

—JEROME ROTHENBERG

MIRROR SUITE

Symbol

Christ,
a mirror
in each hand.
He multiplies
his shadow.
He projects his heart
through his black
visions.
I believe!

The Giant Mirror

We live beneath
a giant mirror.
Man is blue!
Hosanna!

Reflection

Lady Moon.
(Did someone shatter the quicksilver?)
No.
Has a child flicked on
the lantern?
Even a butterfly could
blow you out.
Be quiet!… (Can it really!)
That glowworm
is the moon!

Rays

Everything's a fan.
Brother, open up your arms.
God is the pivot.

Replica

Only a single bird
is singing.
The air is cloning it.
We hear through mirrors.

Earth

We walk on
an unsilvered
mirror,
a crystal surface
without clouds.
If lilies would grow
backwards,
if roses would grow
backwards,
if all those roots
could see the stars
& the dead not close
their eyes,
we would become like swans.

Capriccio

Behind each mirror
is a dead star
& a baby rainbow
sleeping.

Behind each mirror
is a blank forever
& a nest of silences
too young to fly.

The mirror is the wellspring
become mummy, closes
like a shell of light
at sunset.

The mirror
is the mother dew,
the book of desiccated
twilights, echo become flesh.

Shinto

Small golden bells.
Dragon pagoda.
Tinkle tinkle
over the ricefields.

Primal fountain.
Fountain of the real.

Far off,
pink-colored herons
& the spent volcano.

Eyes

In our eyes the roads
are endless.
Two are crossroads of
the shadow.
Death always emerging
from those secret fields.

A woman working a garden:
teardrops like flowers
she breaks.
Horizonless pupils.
Virgin forests
we're lost in.
Castle of no return
that you reach
from the road that starts in the iris.
Oh boy without love, may God
set you free from red ivy.
And you, Elenita,
who sit there
embroidering neckties,
keep clear of that traveler.

Initium

Adam & Eve.
The serpent cracked
the mirror
in a thousand pieces,
& the apple
was his rock.

Berceuse for a Sleeping Mirror

Sleep.
Do not fear the roaming
eye.
Sleep.

The butterfly,
the word,
the furtive light
in through the keyhole,
will not wound you.
Sleep.

As my heart is,
so you are,
my mirror.
Garden where my love
is waiting.

Sleep easy,
but awaken
when the last kiss dies against
my lips.

Air

The air
pregnant with rainbows
shatters its mirrors
over the grove.

Confusion

Is my heart
your heart?
Who is mirroring my thoughts?
Who lends me this un-
rooted passion?
Why are my clothes
changing color?
Everything is a crossroads!
Why does this slime
look so starry?
Brother, are you you
Or am I I?
And these cold hands,
are they his?

I see myself in sunsets
& a swarm of people
wanders through my heart.

The Pool

Horned owl
stops his meditations,
cleans his glasses,
sighs.
A firefly
spins downhill
& a star
slides by.
Old owl shakes his wings,
takes up his meditations.

GARDEN IN UMBER
OR THE GARDEN
OF THE BROWNHAIRED GIRLS

(FRAGMENTS)

Portico

Water
taps its silver
drum.

Trees
knit wind
that roses tint
with scent.

Gigantic
spider
turns moon
into star.

Acacia

Who cut down the moon's
stem?

(Left us roots
of water.)
How easy to pluck flowers from
this infinite acacia.

Encounter

María del Reposo,
again I encounter
thee near the coldspring
hard by the lemongrove.
(Long live the rose on its rosebush!)

María del Reposo,
again I encounter
thee with thy misty hair
& thy eyes of crystal.
(Long live the rose on its rosebush!)

María del Reposo,
again I encounter thee.
Thy moonglove forgotten,
ah where has it gone?
(And long live the rose on its rosebush!)

Lemongrove

Lemongrove.
Flash
in my dream.

Lemongrove.
Nest
of gold
bosoms.

Lemongrove.
Bosom where sucketh
the seabreeze.

Lemongrove.
Orangegrove growing faint,
orangegrove dying,
orangegrove bloodless.

Lemongrove.
You saw my love cracked
by the ax of a grimace.

Lemongrove,
o my child love, my love,
with no crozier, no rose.
O my lemongrove.

NIGHT

(SUITE FOR PIANO AND POET'S VOICE)

Sketches

That road
got no people.
That road.

That weevil
got no home.
That weevil.

And this sheepbell
gone to sleep.
This sheepbell.

Prelude

The bullock
slowly
shuts his eyes.
Heat in the stable.

Prelude to
the night.

In a Corner of the Sky

The old
star
shuts her bleary eyes.

The new
star
wants to paint the night
blue.

(In the firtrees on the mountain:
fireflies.)

The Whole Works

The wind's hand
caresses the forehead of space
again &
again.
The stars half-close
their blue eyelids
again &
agam.

A Star

There is a tranquil star,
a star that has no eyelids.
—Where?
—A star...
In sleepy water.
In the pond.

Swath

O St. James Road.
O Milky Way.
(O night of love for me
when the yellow bird was painted
painted
painted
up in the lemontree.)

One

That romantic star
(one for magnolia,
one for the roses).

That romantic star
just went crazy.

Tralalee,
tralala.

(Sing, little frog,
in your shadowy
hut.)

Ursa Major

Bear mother
gives suck to the stars
astride her belly:
Grunt
grunt.
Run off, star babies,
tender little stars.

Memory

Our Lady Moon still hidden,
playing ring around a wheel.
She makes herself look silly.
Loony moon.

At the Poorhouse

And the poor stars
that have no light

—o sorrow,
sorrow,
o lamentation!—

end up stuck
in muddy blue.

O sorrow,
sorrow,
o lamentation!

Comet

There on Sirius
are babes.

Venus

Open sesame
by day.
Shut sesame
at night.

Below

Space & stars
reflected into sound.
Liana ghosts.
Harp labyrinths.

The Great Sadness

You can't look at yourself
in the ocean.
Your looks fall apart
like tendrils of light.
Night on earth.

BACKWATERS

(Margarita, who am I?)

Cypress.
(Stagnant water.)

Poplar.
(Crystal water.)

Willow.
(Deep water.)

Heart.
(Eyeball water.)

Variation

The backwater of air
under this echo's branches.

The backwater of water
under that frond of stars.

The backwater of your mouth
under our thickening kisses.

Little Backwater

I saw myself in your eyes
& thinking about your soul.

   O oleander white.

I saw myself in your eyes
& thinking about your mouth.

   O oleander red.

I saw myself in your eyes
but saw that you were dead.

   O oleander black.

Song

   Night here already.

Moon's rays been striking
evening like an anvil.

   Night here already.

An old tree keeping warm
wrapped in words of songs.

   Night here already.

If you should come to see me
walking on the air—

   Night here already—

you'd find me crying here
under the poplar trees.

   Ah, morena, my high brown!

Under the poplar trees.

Keep It Going

Each song's
a backwater
of love.

Each star's
a backwater
of time.
Of time tied
in a knot.

And each sigh's
the backwater
of a scream.

Half Moon

Moon goes through the water.
How peaceable the sky is!
Slowly going gathering
old tremors from the river
while a young frog takes her
for a tiny mirror.

     (*Margarita, who am I?*)

CAPRICCIOS

Sun

Sun!
Who was it named you
sun?
No one would be surprised,
I bet,
to see three letters in the sky
instead of your gold
face.

Pirouette

If the alphabet should die
then everything would die.
Whose words are
wings.

The whole of life
dependent on
four letters.

[*Tree*]

Tree
The *tee* gives you leaves

Moon
the *oo* gives you color

Love
the *vee* gives you kisses

Song with Reflections

Out on the prairie my heart
went dancing

(was a cypress's
shadow
out on the wind)

and a tree unbraiding
the breeze from the dew,
the breeze!
silver thing to the touch.

I said: do you remember?

(Not that I cared about
the star
or the rose.)

But, remember?

Word we have lost,
oh horizon-
less word!

Remember?

Out on the prairie my heart
went dancing

(was a cypress's
shadow
out on the wind.)

Unopened Song

Over the river
mosquitoes.

Over the windcurrents
birds.

(Evening adrift.)

Oh this quake
through my heart!

Have no fear,
I'll be going far off
like an echo.

I'll be going far off
in a boat
with no sails
& no oars.

Oh this quake
through my heart!

Sesame

The reflected is
the real.
The river
& sky

are portals that bear us
toward the eternal.
Through streambeds of frogs
or streambeds of stars
our love will go from us, singing
the dawn of the great escape.
The real is
the reflected.
There is only one heart
& one single wind.
Don't you weep! It's the same
from close up
as far out.
Nature: eternal
Narcissus.

Song Under Tears

In that place,
o sweet babe of the fountain,
out there by that brook,
I will take back the rose
my friend gave you.

Out there in that place,
o sweet babe of the fountain,
I will give you my lily.
Why have I cried for so long?
It's so simple!...
And it's just what I'll do, don't you know,
when I be a child once again,
tralala,
when I be a child once again.

At Songfall
      (*Adolfo in 1921*)

After all that

(the moon
opens its tail
of pure gold)

...nada...

(the moon
closes its tail
of pure silver)

Way out there
a star
wounds the peacock
up in the sky.

Landscape Minus Song

Blue sky.
Yellow field.

Blue hill.
Yellow field.

Through the parched prairie
one olive tree
wandering.

One single
tree.

FOUR BALLADS IN YELLOW

For Claudio Guillén

[1]

High up on the mountain
a little green tree

      & a shepherd who comes
      & a shepherd who goes.

Sleepy old olive trees
going down the warm valley

      & a shepherd who comes
      & a shepherd who goes.

Not white ewes nor a dog
nor a sheephook nor love

      for the shepherd who goes.

Like a shadow in gold
you dissolve in the wheat

       you shepherd who comes.

[II]

The earth was
yellow.

       Catch as catch can,
       little shepherd man.

Not a white moon, no
not a star aglow.

       Catch as catch can,
       little shepherd man.

Brown grapepicking woman,
gets tears from the vine.

       Catch as catch can,
       little shepherd man.

[III]
> Two red bulls
> in one gold field.

Bulls got a rhythm
like oldtime bells
& eyes like a bird's.
Made for foggy
mornings, & even so
they bore through the air-
orange, in summer.
Old from their birth
they don't have no boss
& think back to the wings
down their sides.
Two red bulls
that go around sighing
through fields of Ruth
for a shoal to cross over,
that eternal shoal,
drunk on starshine,
are chewing their cuds,
> two red bulls
> in one gold field,
are chewing their sorrows.

46

[IV]

Over a sky
made of daisies
I walk.

I imagine today
that I'm holy.
That they placed the moon
in my hands.
That I set her back
into space.
And the Lord awarded me
a rose & a halo.

Over a sky
made of daisies
I walk.

And now I move
down this field
rescuing maidens from
evil suitors,
giving gold coins
to all the young boys.

Over a sky
made of daisies
I walk.

PALIMPSESTS

For José Moreno Villa

City

A centenary forest
that invades the city
but is a forest set inside
the sea.

And arrows in the air
& warriors who wander
& are lost among its branching
coral boughs.

There, over the new houses,
an oakgrove has started moving,
& the sky's there with enormous
crystal curves.

Corridor

Through the vaulted corridors
two gentlemen stroll by.

>   (*New*
>   *sky.*
>   *Blue*
>   *sky!*)

...two gentlemen stroll by
who once were two white monks.

>   (*Mid*
>   *sky.*
>   *Mauve*
>   *sky!*)

...two gentlemen stroll by
who once were two white hunters.

>   (*Old*
>   *sky.*

Gold
       sky!)

…two gentlemen stroll by
who once were…

       (*Night.*)

Air

Full of scars
& fast asleep.
And full of spirals,
signs.
The wake behind a bird
& the wake behind a scream.
Out from the whirligig
of words & rhythms,
two sounds break loose:
a black, a yellow.

Madrigal

Oh Lucy of Granada!
my little brownhaired girl,
who lives down by the foot of the Red
Towers...what if your hands?
...your hands...

(full moon)

Oh girl of April!
Melisendra!
You of the high towers
& the spindle.
What if your breasts! ...your breasts...

(half moon)

Oh woman of my snowwhite
adolescence!
Striped & fecund
Eve,
how in my arms you twist

like the dry branches
of an oaktree, in the bonfire's
dance.

(And my heart?
was it wax?
Where is it?
…& my hands?
&?…)

(blind moon)

Front Page

For Isabel Clara, my goddaughter

Clear fountain.
Clear sky.

Oh how the birds
grow bigger!

Clear sky.
Clear fountain.

Oh how the oranges
shine!

Fountain.
Sky.

Oh how the corn
is tender!

Sky.
Fountain.

Oh how the corn
is green!

THREE PRINTS OF THE SKY

Dedicated to Señorita Argimira López, who didn't love me

[1]

The stars
don't have a lover—

doesn't matter how pretty
the stars are!

They will wait for
their heartthrob—
to carry them off to
his perfect Venezia.

Every night they'll slip out
to their railings
—o thousand-tiered sky—
& make lyrical gestures
at the ocean of shadows
around them.

But wait up, muchachas!
Because when I die
I will drag you away,
one by one,
on my cloudcovered pony.

[II]

Heartthrob

In that whole big sky
there is only one boy star.

Romantic & crazy.
With a top hat & tails
lined with gold
dust.

(But he tracks down a mirror,
he does, to gaze at his body.

Oh silver Narcissus,
riding high in the water.)

In that whole big sky
there is only one boy star.

[III]

Venus

Sure enough,
you've got two big boobs
& a necklace of pearls
on your neck.

A child of the mist
holds your mirror.

Though you're very far off
I still see you,
placing a hand like a rainbow's
over your sex
or lazily punching the sky
into shape, like a pillow.

We're looking at you through a lens—
the renaissance & me.

SEASIDE PRINTS

To Emilio and Manolo

The sea
wants to blow
its lid.
Coral giants
heave with
their shoulders.

And in their gold caverns
the sirens
try out a song
that the water can sleep to.
Do you see its gullet
& scales?
In front of the sea
raise your lances.

Contemplation

I evoke
the Corinthian capital,
the fallen column,
the pines.
The classical sea
that sings ever in summer
& like the Corinthian
capital, trembles.

Nocturne

I stare at the stars
that are over the ocean.
Oh stars made of water,
oh water drops.

I stare at the stars
that are over my heart.
Oh stars made of odors,
oh nuclei of odors.

I stare at the earth
filled with shadows.

The Guardsmen

In the kingdom of the sea
are two guards:
St. Christopher
& Polyphemus.
Three eyes over
the vagabond rover.

The Sea with Two Stars

In Daybreak
Tower
Mary shows Venus
how to knit wool.
Venus shows Mary all
her best features.
And Mary's left speechless.
            In Daybreak
            Tower.

TWILIGHT HOURS

3:00 p.m.

The air from the west
will already be stirring.

A yellow sea 's
covering earth.
And a man made of gold 's
bathing down by the river,
while sun 's come to ruin
in the molten blue sky.

—The air from the west
will already be stirring.—

[...]

*

Scissor man.
(3:00 p.m.)
Soul of Pan on
the lips of
the scissor man.
So much sadness
such dust!

He calls forth
a green pool
& a zither
up in the branches.

Man who carries
a catherine
wheel.

Ah so much sadness!

6:00 p.m.

Birds jab at
the evening,
beaks carrying off
day's blue tail.

Sunset tattooed with
weathercocks
props up the half moon's
small boat.

And in the cold fountain
the little snake sings.

7:00 p.m.

First star out.
Everything looking toward Venus,
& she like a girl
who falls down a deep well,
shivers & shakes—
as if she was saying
"will I come back tomorrow?"

8:00 p.m.

Sky tears off
the blindfold
& the thousand-eyed dragon
licks us all over with
windtongues.

Venus wandering off
through the crowd
& I thinking back to a sweetheart
I never did have.

9:00 p.m.

A bloodless blue sky.
And a velvety breeze.

Oh my lady!

We can
make our way down to the cistern,
the heart, down

this river of words,
we can
come to

Kiss Island,
can
sink out of sight in
that burntover
olive grove.

[I]

The wind came in red
through the burntover pass
& changed into green
down by the river.
And will change into violet
yellow & (what?).
Over fields sown with seed,
an elongated rainbow.

[II]

Stagnant wind.
Sun above you.
Below you
the tremulous algae of
aspens.
And my heart
trembling too.

Stagnant wind
at five in the afternoon
& no birds.

[III]

The breeze
so wavy
like the hair of
certain girls.
Like the oceans made small
in certain old panels.
The breeze
now gushes like water,
now overflows
—tenuous balsamic white—
through the canebrakes,
now faints,
where it crashes against
this rock of a mountain.

[IV]

School

The Teacher
What maiden will marry
the wind?

The Child
The maiden of all
our desires.

The Teacher
What does the wind
give the maiden?

The Child
Whirlwinds of gold.
A pileup of maps.

The Teacher
And she gives him what?

The Child
Her heart laid bare.

The Teacher
Tell me her name.

The Child
Her name is a secret.

> (The window
> in the school
> has a curtain
> of stars.)

FAIRS

A Poem at the Fairground

Tuba's a sun & beneath it
the fair's passing by,
see it breathing out old
captive Pegasuses.

This fair
is a wheel.
A lightwheel high up
in the night.

See the carousel making
concentric circles,
see them snake through the atmosphere
up to the moon.

And a boy all the poets
have lost,
& a music box grinding away
on the breeze.

Song in Brown

I would lose myself
in your brown country,
María del Carmen,

would lose myself there
in your eyes (sans people),
would play on those keys,
your incredible mouth.

In our endless embrace
the air would be brown
& the breeze like
the down on your skin.

I would lose myself there
in your quivering breasts,
in your easy body's
deep darkness.

I would lose myself
in your brown country,
María del Carmen.

[…]

SUBLUNAR CANTOS

Full Moon
(At Moonrise)

When the moon comes out
the bells get lost
& the paths we can't cross
come in sight.

When the moon comes out
ocean covers the earth
& heart feels like
infinity's island.

Moon more distant
than the sun & stars.
Is perfume & memory,
faded blue bubble.

Colors

Over Paris the moon's
got a violet color
& yellow
in the dead cities.

There's a green moon
that's moon of the legends,
a spiderweb moon
& a cracked stained glass moon,
& over the deserts
a deep bloody moon.

But the white moon,
the true moon,
only shines on the soundless
graves in small towns.

Capriccio

In the net of moon,
the sky spider,
stars get entangled,
spinning around.

Salome & the Moon

The moon is Salome's
sister. (Lady
who in the old story
gnaws a dead mouth.)

Salome was sunset.
Sunset
of eyes
& of lips.

Moon is perpetual
sunset.
Evening
unending &
frantic.

Love without bounds
of Salome for gold
—or for John—
was not for his word
but his head,
that desert medusa,
was now a black moon,
an impossible moon,
filled with smoke,
lost in sleep.

Salome the chrysalis
& moon the cocoon,
this shadowy chrysalis
beneath a dark palace.

Moon trembling over the water,
Salome over the soul.
Oh beauty sublime!
that would turn a kiss into
a star.

In the midst of the day
or the dark night,
if you speak of Salome
the moon will come out.

[...]

SHADOW

Pueblo

Flows between roof & roof
the sky-high river.

Atop old acacias
migrant birds fast asleep.

And the tower with no bells
(St. Lucy in stone)
standing firm in hard earth.

Memento

When we die
we'll take with us
a series of shots
of the sky.

(Skies around daybreak
& skies in the night.)

Though they've told me
that dead
we don't have any memories
past a sky in midsummer,
a black sky
shaken up
by the wind.

Bat

Bat,
elixir of shadows,
true love of that star,
nips at day's heel.

End

End of the world
has already happened
& Terrible Judgment
has been.

Already demise of the stars
has occurred.

Night sky is
a wilderness—
a desert of lamps
with no owner.

Silver crowds
gone astray
in the thickening yeast of
the Mystery.

In the ship of Death
we are traveling, feeling
we're playing at life,
that we're ghosts!

Looking in all four directions
everything's dead.
Night sky is
a ruin,
an echo.

Ursa Major
   (We were seven.
    Where are we?)

A Toy

Makes me feel sad,
seeing that cart
without any driver
or horses.

Over the sky
there's a lingering
sadness: to see how you're dreaming
a road paved with gold
& boreal horses.

Over that crystalline blackness
what will you do, cart,
when the rainy days have
rusted your stars?
Will you think, ever, to pack it in
under a roof?

One day I might yoke you
to two big white bulls.

Sundown

On this exquisite sky,
& long past the violet
the clouds lie shredded
like gray camellias—
a desire for wings
atop the cold mountains.

A sunset that's tinted
with shadows like this one
will call forth a vast night
sans breeze, sans highways.

Mountaintop

Coming up to the mountaintop...

(Desolate heart,
St. Sebastian of Eros.)

Coming up to the mountaintop...

Let me sing!
Because singing
I will not see the shadowy buttes
or the flock
in the depths
with no shepherds.
Singing
I will see the one star
that doesn't exist.

Coming up to the mountaintop...
singing.

Willow

Exquisite
Jeremiah!

Tears shine forth
through your very cold eyes
but your sobs do not roll
down this highway.

Under your branches you open
a gulf
& your gestures add shades to
the color of vespers.

O exquisite
Jeremiah!

THE RETURN

I'm coming back
for my wings.

O let me come back!

I want to die where
it's dawn!

I want to die where
it's yesterday!

I'm coming back
for my wings.

O let me get back!

I want to die where
it's origin.

I want to die
out of sight
of the sea.

In Motion

You walk,
you get muddy.

Water in motion
will not see the stars.

You walk,
you go blank.

You stop walking,
you dream.

Towards. . .

Turn,
corazón!
turn.

Through forests where love is
you won't see a soul.
You will come on sweet waters.

Out where it's green
you will spot the great rose
named forever.
And will call out: Love! love!
without your wound
closing

Turn,
mi corazón!
turn.

Oxbow

I want to go back to childhood
& from childhood to shadow.

You going too, nightingale?
Better get going!

I want to go back to the shadow
& from the shadow to the flower.

You going too, perfume?
Better get going!

I want to go back to the flower
& from the flower
to my heart.

You going too, love?
Adios.

My bare heart.

Saying Goodbye

I'll be saying goodbye
at the crossroads,
heading off down that road
through my soul.

I'll arouse reminiscences,
stir up mean hours.
I'll arrive at the garden spot

in my song (my white song),
& I'll start in to shiver & shake
like the morning star.

Wind Gust

My girl coming by,
how sweet she looks walking!
with her cute muslin
dress
& a newly caught
butterfly.

Trail her, muchacho,
down every byway,
& if you once catch her crying
or thinking it over,
paint this onto her heart
& spray it with glitter
& tell her not to cry
if she should stay single.

IN THE FOREST OF CLOCKS

I entered the forest
of clocks.

Leaves were ticking,
bells hung in clusters.
Under a many-faced clock,
constellations and pendulums.

Black iris,
dead hours.
Black iris,
new hours.
All the same!
And love's golden hour?

There is only one hour,
one hour.
A very cold hour.

Chaparral

I plunged into my
hour of death.
My death rattle hour.
Hour of last kisses.
Grave hour the captive bells
dream of.

Cuckoo clocks
without cuckoos.
Mildewing star
& enormous pale
butterflies.

From brambles
of sighs
the crank organ
sounded
that I had as a child.

You must skip to my loo,
my darling,
skip to my loo,
my love.

Overview

The whole murky forest is one
giant spider
spinning a soundweb
for hope:
this poor lilywhite girl,
raised on glances & sighs.

He

The real sphinx
is a clock.

Oedipus will be born from its eye.
Its northern boundary
is mirror.
Its southern is cat.

Doña Luna is Venus.

Savorless sphere.

Clocks bring us
winter.

(Hieratic swallows,
they migrate in summer.)
Dawn is a floodtide
of clocks
where the dream is drowned.

Bats born from
spheres.

And the bullcalf scans them
heavy with thought.

When will nightfall come
for all these clocks?
When will those white moons sink
under their hills?

Clock Echo

I sat down
in a clearing in time.
It was a pool of silence.
White silence.
Incredible ring
where the bright stars collide
with a dozen floating
black numbers.

First/Last Meditation

Time
is in night's colors.
Quiet night.
Over enormous moons,
eternity
is set at twelve.
Time's gone to sleep
forever
in his tower.

All clocks
deceive us.
Time at last has
horizons.

The Sphinx Hour

In your garden the damned
stars open up.
We're born under your horns
& die there.
Cold hour!
You drop a stone roof
on these lyrical butterflies:
propped up in your sky
you cut off their wings
& confine them.

★

[...]

One... two... three.
The hour struck in the forest.
The silence
filled up with bubbles.
A gold pendulum
carried my face
through the air.
The hour struck in the forest!
Pocket watches,
squadrons of flies,
came & went.

From my heart came the sound
of my grandmother's
goldplated watch.

WHITE ALBUM

For Claudio de la Torre

Eloísa López kept an album in which she didn't write. And she died. Poor little thing! But I wrote something for her with white ink. I ask those who read it to pray for her soul. The Archbishop of Constantinople has deigned to grant 100 days of indulgence. Ah! if only you had known her...

First Page
(Cherry tree in flower)

In March
you go off to the moon.
Leave your shadow behind.
The prairies are turning
unreal.
They're raining white birds.
And I'm stuck in your forest
& cry

"Open sesame!"
(Could I still be a child?)
"Open sesame!"

Second Page
(Cygnus/The Swan)

Not Pan
& not Leda.

(The full moon
sleeps over your wings.)

Not forest
& not syrinx.

(Through your feathers
cold night slipping by.)

Not blond flesh
& not kisses.

(Made of frost & of dreams, you
towing a boat for the dead.)

Third Page
(Conjurations)

(Snow stars)

There are mountains
that want to be
water
& that conjure up stars
over their shoulders.

(Clouds)

And there are mountains
that want to have
wings
& that conjure up clouds,
like white clouds.

Fourth Page
(*Snow*)

The stars
stripping down:
now blouses of stars
line the fields.

Fifth Page
(*At Dawn*)

Day's crest
first appearing,
white crest
of a goldcolored cock.

Crest of my laugh
first appearing.
Gold crest
of a shadowy cock.

Final Page
Little ballad for dead Eloísa
(in the words of a student)

You were dead,
Eloísa,
like the dead at the end of all
novels.
I never did love you,
sweet as you were!
With music by Bécquer
or by Espronceda,
you dreamt of me handsome
& longhaired,
I who was kissing you
& was never aware
that I still had not told you
"oh lips like a cherry!"
What an awful romantic
you were,
drank down in secret
your grandmother's vinegar,
became like a tree,

a mockorange, in springtime.
And I was in love
with another.
        (See how it hurts?)
With another I wrote out
a name in the sand.

When I got to your house
you were dead,
among candles & basil.
Just like in those novels.
Your poor boat encircled
by the girls from your school.
You had drunk of the vinegar,
the perpetual bottle.

Baby Doll

Why do I remember you,
a rainy day in March,
coming out of the convent?

Little white snowbird
they called you. A schoolboy
once gave you his rose. Then
a feather dropped from you
with which I am writing these verses.
Such a small thing & you
will not know it!

SIX SONGS AT NIGHTFALL

Horizon

From above the green mist
old sun plunges down
sans sunrays.

And the shadowy shore
dreams in time to a boat
& a bell you can't miss
joins its sorrows.

In my leftover soul
there's the sound of a small
silver drum.

Fishermen

Gigantic tree,
with its lianas, fishes
rare moles
from the earth.

Above the pond the willow
fishes nightingales
...but on the cypress's green
fishhook, white moon
will not bite...nor will
your heart on mine,
oh brunette of Granada.

Solitaire
(Zujaira)

Over the pianissimo
of gold...
my lonely
poplar.

Without some harmonical
bird.

Over the pianissimo of gold...

The river at its feet
runs dark & deep
beneath the pianissimo
of gold…

And I with evening
on my shoulders
like a little lamb
the wolf has slain
beneath the pianissimo
of gold.

Delirium

Evening come apart
& the field gone silent.
The bee-eaters
flying past, sighing.
In the distances: wild
blues & whites.
The landscape with arms
spread wide open.
(Oh, lordy, lordy! if
this ain't too much.)

Memento
(Prairie Air)

The moon is dead already
       do-re-mi
we're going to bury her now
       do-re-fa
in a chalk white rose
       do-re-mi
with a bright glass stalk
       do-re-fa.
She went down 'mongst the poplars
       do-re-mi
got tangled in the briars
       do-re-fa.
I am happy about it because she
       do-re-mi
thought she was something special
       do-re-fa.
Nobody was good enough to be
       do-re-mi
her husband or her lover
       do-re-fa.
How happy the sky is going to be
       do-re-mi

yes how happy the sky is going to be
  do-re-fa
when the night has come around
  do-re-mi
& doesn't see her in the ocean
  do-re-fa.
Let us all go to her funeral
  do-re-mi
& let's sing the pío pa
  do-re-fa.
La Mambruna's stone cold dead
  do-re-mi
with her face that's like a star
  do-re-fa.
So let bells from their towers
  do-re-mi
ring like mad & ring like mad
  do-re-fa.
And let snakes at their fountains
  do-re-mi
sing like mad & sing like mad
  do-re-fa!

Last Light

In blue
confusion
distant bonfire
(skewering the mountain's
heart).
Birds who play at wind
amongst the poplars
& streambeds growing deeper
deeper down.

Snows

Field got no roads
& town got no roofs.
A silent & pale
world.
Gigantic dove
in the stars.
(Why don't he come down from the sky,
that perpetual buzzard?)

Worlds

Perpetual angle
of earth & sky,
with wind the bisector.

Enormous angle,
the road going straight,
with sex the bisector.

The parallels meet
in a kiss.
Oh heart without
echoes.
In you the beginning & end
of the All.

[...]

Homeland

Trees laid out
in black water,

daisies &
poppies.

Down the dead highway
come three oxen.

Nightingales
aloft,
heart of the tree.

Tremor

Dark to my mind,
with just a memory of silver,
a stone of dew.

In that field no mountain.
Only a clear lake,
a snuffed out spring.

Acacia

Who cut down the moon's
stem?
Left us roots
of water.
How easy to pluck flowers from
this infinite acacia.

Curve

With a lily in your hand
I leave you,
o my night love!
Little widow of my single star
I find you.

Tamer of dark
butterflies!
I keep along my way.
After a thousand years are gone
you'll see me,
o my night love!

By the blue footpath,
tamer of dark
stars,
I'll make my way.
Until the universe
can fit inside
my heart.

[...]

Beehive

We live in crystal
cells,
in a beehive made of air!
Kiss each other through
the glass.
Marvelous prison house,
whose gateway is
the moon!

CROSS

North

Cold stars
over our highways.
Those who come & those who go
through smoky forests.
The way the cabins breathe
beneath an endless dawn.
With each hit
the axe makes
valleys & forests quake
like cisterns.
With each hit
the axe makes!

South

South,
mirage,
reflection.
Might as well say star
as orange.
Riverbed as sky.
Oh arrow
arrow!
is what the South
is:
golden arrow
with no bullseye,
rides the wind.

East

Diapason of fragrances
drops
South
(by set degrees).

West

Diapason of moon
climbs
North
(chromatic).

THREE CREPUSCULAR POEMS

For my sister Conchita

[I]

The evening is
penitent,
still dreaming about
noon.
(Red trees & clouds
over the hills.)
The evening, loosening green
lyric hair,
is gently trembling
...vexed
to be the evening having once been
noon.

[II]

Now the evening starts!
Why? Why?

...just now
I watched the day droop down
just like a morning flower.
A day lily
bending its stems
...just now...
the roots of evening
rising through the gloom.

[III]

(For Diane Rothenberg)

Adiós, sun!

I know for sure that you're the moon,
but I
won't tell nobody,
sun.

You sneak
behind the curtain
& cover your face
with rice powder.

By day, the farmhand's
guitar,
by night, Pierrot's
mandolin.

I should care!

Your illusion,
sun, is to make
the garden
turn Technicolor.

Adiós, sun!

And don't forget who loves you:
the snail,
the little old lady
on her balcony,
& me...
spinning my heart like a...
top.

[BLUE RIVER]

Blue river.
An ivory boat
carries apples.
Dead kisses.
Snow apples,
furrows atremble from lips.
Blue river.
And the water
stares out, liquid—
branch of an infinite
eye.
River blue.

Dreams

My whole dream shuts down tight
the way an old
star
might shut down
so as not to spill
its last light.

The outside of
my whole dream painted
with my empty
words.

My dream!
My granary of stars
with its gold
worms.
My dream!
A smalltown promenade,
an empty bench.
My Lady Honeyhead
who rolls
her hundred eyes—
a shady form
moves down the highway
with the rain.

My whole dream shuts down tight.

Lianas from the blue
touch my forehead.
Hazy limbs

on Yahveh's old
firtrees
darken the virgin
horizon.

Divine perturbation
of the blue sky in ruins.
Stars fallen
on moon's balding head.
Tufts of unreal vegetation.
Other stars
burst their shells.
And a new heaven's seed
is embedding itself in a frost
that won't end.

My heart
fills with
wings!
An army
of memories lost
on Death's road.

On the rose
leaf,
the earth,
under this unreal forest
I stride.
Little man
with no story to tell,
no desire.

Lonesome Blues

I toss off my clothes
& squeeze my heart dry.
Heart oozes mist.
When sky's woods hide
earth's,
my heart will still be
soaked with mist.

    Blue river.
I look for my long-ago kiss.

That kiss from my own
little hour.
My mouth, a dead
lamp,
still looks for its light.

      Blue river.
These great heaps
of kisses,
molds of botched mouths.
These unending kisses,
like snails stuck tight to
an ivory mast.

And so the boat stops.
There's a rhythmless peace
& I scamper on deck
tricked out like a poet.

But those weird kisses,
choke me.
Soap bubbles,
the soul manufactures

while mine's flying off
through the cold
northern ashes.

    Blue river.

[SUITE]

[...]

Those Who Wait

My old body
& my old soul
are waiting for me.

(Where the rivers
open their hands.)

Without lanterns
& glowworms—
with shadows.

(Where an arm of
the river
opens its hand.)

My old body
flashing me signs
from in back of a spiderweb.

(Signs from ocean's
umbilicus.)

Landscape Seen with the Nose

A cold tremor
burnt out of flesh by
the roosters
drops a cloud on the prairie.
In the house
someone's burning
the chaff.
The plows will come
with the dawn.

Sphere

It's the same if it's
river or geyser
because both go up
to the stars.

It's the same if it's
ridge or ravine
because both lie under
the shadow.

Sundown

The sun
when it's sundown
digs into your gut
like an x-ray.
Opens up the façades
& discolors
the glass at your heart.
Be careful!

The air is invading your secret's
sinister rooms
& your words in bondage
loom up in your eyes.
And that's why the prudent
rooster
will lock up his hens
around twilight.

[...]

*

[............]

What's coming up?
What's not coming up?

Colorized parsley &
sleepy old oil lamps.

What's coming up?
What's not coming up?

Hermit gets sleepy
& princess
gets sleepy, even their story
gets sleepy!

What's coming up?
What's not coming up?

THE PALM TREE
A TROPICAL POEM

Limits

Star in the sky—
& octopus below.
(Satan's palm tree
& Zoroaster's.)
The star floats
in space.
The octopus floats in
the Mediterranean.
Satan's palm tree
& Zoroaster's
sway
when their arms vibrate.

Palm Tree

Between water & sky
you expose your large flower.
Living rose of the Mediterranean
wind.

With your hairdo of dates,
a Negress's graces,
you evoke a contemplative
gorgon.

You are there by the waves
like a spider-stork
weaving its rhythms of salt
& iodine

dreaming how under its
tentative foot   in the sand
there's a country of blue
oases.

Mediterranean

Latin sea!
palm trees
& olives!

The cry of the palm
or the pine tree's silence.

I feel your sound like
an overblown column
climbing higher than all other
seas.
Latin sea!
(Between whitewashed towers
& Corinthian capitals,

skidding across you,
came Jesus Christ's voice.)
Latin sea!

The sky's fat penis
gave you its heat. Your rhythm
flows out in concentric waves
from Venus, your omphalos.
Latin sea!

You strike immortal poses
& are humble. I have seen
blind sailors sail forth
& return to their lot.
Oh Peter, patron of seas!
Oh magnificent
desert crowned with
palm trees & olives.

The Palm

The palm is air.
Neither river nor Eve
could form curves
so perfect.

The palm is gold.
Neither lemon nor wheat
could go further
from yellow.

The palm is Grace.
In our hands
it attains the blue summit
of swooning.

★

Onto the nose of Newton
a large apple falls.
A meteor of truths.
Last fruit to dangle from
the tree of Science.
And big Newton scratches
his Saxon nostrils.
A white moon over
these barbaric strings of lace:
the beech trees.

In the Woods

The gnomes
astride their secrets
tear
their beards out.
They tie up Death

& make the Echoes
mislead men
with mirrors.
In a corner
lies the secret,
in the open,
dead.
A blue boy
with iron feet—
a glowing star
between his eyebrows.
His companions
mourn him.
And the green lake trembles.
In the wind.

Harmony

Waves
rhyme with sighs
& stars with
crickets.

Atremble in the cornea
the whole cold sky.
A dot, a synthesis,
infinity's.
But who joins waves
with sighs?
And stars
with crickets?
Just hope these genies
may be missing something.
The proofs keep drifting by
among us.

The Philosopher's Last Walk

Newton
was taking a walk.
Death had followed him,
strumming his guitar.
Newton
was taking a walk.
The worms gnawed through
his apple.

The wind hummed in the trees,
the river beneath the branches.
(Wordsworth would have cried.)
The philosopher was striking
unimaginable poses,
was waiting for another apple.
He ran along the road.
He stretched out by the water.
He saw how his face would sink
in the big moon's reflection.
Newton
wept.

And high up on a cedar two
old owls yammered.
Slowly in the night the wise man
went back home.
He dreamt enormous pyramids
of apples.

Reply

Adam ate an apple
from the Virgin Eve.
Newton was a second Adam—
Science's.
The first knew
Beauty.
The second a Pegasus
bowed down by chains.
And neither one was guilty.
Their two apples
pink
& fresh
but with a bitter
history.
The severed breasts of
innocence, poor child.

Question

Why was it the apple
& not
the orange
or the polyhedral
pomegranate?
Why this virgin fruit
to clue them in,
this smooth & gentle
pippin?
What admirable symbol
lies dormant at its core?
Adam, Paris, Newton
carry it inside their souls
& fondle it without a clue
to what it is.

CÚCKOO-CUCKOO-CUCKÓO

For Enrique Díez-Canedo & Teresa

The cuckoo divides the night
with its tiny copper pellets.

The cuckoo has no beak,
only two little lips like a child's
to whistle the centuries home.

Cat,
hide your cat tail!

The cuckoo flies over time,
floating in space like a sailboat
splitting apart like an echo.

Magpie,
hide your bird foot!

In front of the cuckoo's the sphinx
the symbol of the swan,

& the little girl who won't laugh.

Fox lady,
hide your fox tail!

One day it's all gone with the wind
the absolutely last thought
& the next to the last desire.

Cricket,
get under that pine!

For only the cuckoo will stay
splitting eternity
with its tiny crystal pellets.

The Old Cuckoo's Song

In Noah's ark
I did sing.
And down on Methusaleh's farm.

For Noah was one good hombre.
And Methusaleh's
beard touched
the ground.

He launched my whistles
up to the sky. I got them
to fall down empty
just one more time.

Over the night I did sing.
I will sing
though you be asleep.
Por todos los siglos
de los siglos.
Time without end. Amen.

Cuckoo's First Nocturne

In despite of his eyes
the night's getting lost.

(For only the cuckoo
endureth.)

In the canebrake the sobbing
of uncertain winds.

(For only the cuckoo
endureth.)

Here? There? The soul
's lost power of smell.

(For only the cuckoo
endureth.)

Cuckoo's Second Nocturne

The cuckoo says Yes.
Get happy, goldfinch!
Angel opens the gates
to his garden.

The cuckoo says No.
Sing out, little nightingale!
With a flower
in each eye.
Oh what a great
resurrection!

And it's No!
And it's Yes!

(The night
back to the confines of Night.)

And it's Yes!
And it's No!

(Clock dribbles waterdrops
time winding down.)

Last Nocturne

Oh what a shuddering!
Cuckoo's come to town,
let's all of us clear out!

If you should see the bitter
oleander sobbing,
what would you do, amor mío?

I would think about the ocean.

If you were to see the moon
call you as it floats away,
what would you do, amor mío?

Sigh.

And if one day I was to say:
"I love you" from my olive grove,
what would you do, amor mío?

Stick a dagger in myself.

Oh what a shuddering!
Cuckoo's come to town,
let's all of us clear out!

DAYDREAMS OF A RIVER

(Rio Genil)

The poplars are fading away
but leave their reflections.

      (What a beautiful
      time!)

The poplars are fading away
but leave us the wind.

The wind's shrouding everything
under the sun.

      (What a sad little
      time!)

But it leaves us its echoes,
afloat on the river.

The world of the fireflies
has invaded my thoughts.

                (What a beautiful
                    time!)

And a miniature heart
blossoms on my fingers.

*

This backwash has lotuses
spread in concentric circles.
On my temples I bear their
majestical silence.

Marvelous bevels shatter
the poplar trees.
Through the grass on the riverbank
little white snails come & go.

Lazy River

Down the river my eyes drift away
down the river…
Down the river my love drifts away
down the river…
(My heart goes on counting
how long it's asleep.)
The river is bearing dead leaves,
the river…
The river is crystal & deep,
the river…
(And my heart asks me
can it change places.)

[…]

MADRIGALS

[1]

Like concentric waves
on the water,
your words
in my heart.

Like a bird that collides
with the wind,
your kiss
on my lips.

Like open fountains
fronting the night,
my dark eyes
on your skin.

[II]

I'm caught
in your concentric
circles.
Like Saturn
I lug around
rings
from my dreams.
I'm not totally sunk,
I'm not rising.
My love!
But my body's
afloat on this bayou,
your kisses.

MEDITATIONS & ALLEGORIES
OF WATER

For many years now—being a smalltime dreamer
& an easygoing guy—I have spent my summers at
a cool spot down along a river. In the afternoons,
when those amazing birds, the bee-eaters, start
singing in anticipation of the wind & an angry
cicada rubs its two gold plates together, I sit down
beside a deep & active pool & move my eyes around
until they settle, frightened, on the water or the
rounded treetops of the nearby poplars.

Under some spiky osiers, up by the water's edge,
I feel the afternoon come open, gently pressing
against the pool's green surface. A silent air begins
to freeze the astonished crystal in my eyes.

For the first few days the spectacle of what I saw
reflected there enthralled me: the fallen poplar
groves that changed to solomonic columns at the
slightest stirring of the water, the brambles & the
reeds that curled up like a nun's cloth.

I didn't notice that my soul was changing to a prism, that it was filling with immense perspectives, trembling phantoms. One afternoon, while staring at the mobile greenness of the waves, I saw how a strange gold bird had curved itself around a reflected poplar. But when I looked hard at the tree's real leaves awash with sunset, only some invisible small windbirds played in them. The golden bird had disappeared.

A marvelous coolness took hold of my body, as if to bind me with the last strands of the sunset's hair, & a broad avenue of light ran through my heart. How could this be? My soul on a trip through the waves instead of a flight to the stars?

A sheep bell left dark echoes in my throat & I felt my soul's amazing skin being spattered by small crystal drops. O soul, why didn't you stay true to Venus's quavering or to the wind's violin? why the sonorous algae in the waterfalls & the enormous flower the concentric circle makes?... And I saw all my memories reflected!

Border

I was returning from the high desert. Down below a river valley trembled, wrapped in blue. Out of the summer night, the sprawling air, some cricket ribbons, trembling, floated.

The desert music has a truly yellow taste.

I know now why cicadas are made of solid gold & how a song can turn to ashes in the olive groves.

Dead bodies living in these distant cemeteries must turn as yellow as November trees.

Getting close to the valley, we seemed to have entered a green fishtank: the air was a sea of blue waves, an ocean made for the moon, where frogs play on multiple flutes of dry cane.

To get from the desert to the valley, you cross a mysterious ford that few people notice: the Ford of Sounds. This ford forms a natural boundary where an eerie silence tries to stifle two contradictory musics. If our spiritual eyes were made for it, we would discern how a man, turned yellow by the desert gold, changes to green on entering the valley, after disappearing in the murky flow of music at the border.

What man can travel this long road & not fill up his soul with crazy arabesques? Who would dare say "I walked along a road in my head, & it wasn't a road for birds or for fish or for men, but a road for our ears"?

Is this the road that leads to Nowhere, the home of those who died of waiting? From the rear of the olive grove to the advance line of poplars, what fantastic algae & little invisible lights float around us!

Here I would pause beside the current & with my ears as antennae would explore its depths. The ford is wide & full of whirlpools, while in the mountains it is buried under the blue desert sand. Now it has the wonderful confusion of forgotten dreams.

The waning moon, like a clove of gold garlic, scatters down from a young boy's face on a curve in the sky.

BARRAGE OF FIREWORK POEMS
ON THE OCCASION
OF THE POET'S BIRTHDAY

First Launching

You you you you
me me me me
Who?...
not you!
not me!

Catherine Wheel

Doña Catalina
had a single gold hair
among her shadowy
tresses.

(For whom am I waiting,
dear God,
for whom am I waiting?)

Doña Catalina
walks slowly
scattering little green stars
in the night.

(Not here
& not there
but here.)

Doña Catalina:
a grenade of light
dies & is born
on her forehead.

chsssssssssssss!

Rockets

Six fiery spears
zoom up.
(The night's a guitar.)
Six fuming serpents.

(St. George will dive through the sky.)
Six torches of gold & of wind.
(Will they puff up the bell jars
of night?)

Chinese Garden

In the little woodlets
with their purples & magnesiums
the princesitas jumping
are baby sparkadillos.

There's a rain of oranges
above the zigzag cherryos—
& between commas comes a flight
of prancing blue dragondolas.

My little girl this gardenette's
best looked at in the mirrorettes
that are thy fingernails.
And in those screens that are thy teeth.
As by a little mouselet.

Sunflower

If I did love a cyclops
I would swoon
beneath his stronger gaze
sans eyelids.
O fiery sunflower, ay!
The people stare at it
sans shuddering.
Eyeball of Providence
eyeing a crowdful of
Abels!

Sunflower sunflower!
Pure savage eyeball
sans winkage sans irony!

Sunflower sunflower!
Stigmata raging above
a fair full of peoples.

The Ruby Disc

gyrates & shakes
like crazy.
Knowing nothing—
knows it all?
All those arrows aimed
at this round
heart.
All those eyeballs aimed
at this round
heart.
A bloody lens between
the mystery
& us.

Capriccio

    Zip!...
Did you just close
your eyes?
    Ziiip!...

Even more? That's a
breezy young girl.
And I am an hombre.
        Zap!
Already you're gone, o my love,
& your eyes?
        Zaaap!…
If you close them, I have here two feathers,
you hear? two feathers staring out
from my peacock.
        Zip!
Did you hear me?
        Zaaap!…

A Game of Moons

Moon is round.
Roundabout it is a treadmill
built with mirrors.
Roundabout it is a wheel
like a waterwheel.
Moon's become a gilt leaf

like a loaf of white gold.
Moon sheds its petals
like moons.
Swarms of fountains
float through the sky.
In each fountain's a moon
lying dead.
Moon
becomes a cane made of light
in bright torrents.
Moon
like a large stained glass window
that breaks on the ocean.
Moon
through an infinite
screen.
And the moon? And the moon?

(Up
above nothing left but a ring
of small crystals.)

WHEELS OF FORTUNE

Fan-tan

Chance's
zodiac
opens up, fanlike
red yellow green.

In the forest of numbers
a little girl lost
's got closed eyes
four? five? seven?

Each number's enclosing
a bird or a snake.
Yes says the four
No says the twenty.

On a sky ruled by chance
the little girl's finger
pins up her star—
most rich present.

Roulette

Rose
with the deepdown corolla.
Is it so hard to swallow
that pinball?

You've got a sky
of fake jewels
& fleshless hands
strip you blind.

With blurred eyes
you whirl by
the bitter
inquisitor's garden.

Sleepless & cold
you whirl by.
Fanning out your great tail
like a peacock of numbers.

CARACOLS/SNAILS

Caracol, now
hold still.

Where you are
will be center.

Stone over water
& cry in the wind
forming the pure
imagings in your dreams,
impossible circumferences
inside your body.

Caracol col col col
now be quiet.

White Caracols

The children play under
the poplar trees.
The little old river
runs very slowly,
seating itself on green
chairs, in the backwaters.
Where'd be my child, then?
Child who would change to a horse.
Tinkle tinkle! My child,
little madman! is singing,
would like to escape
my closed heart.

Sweet little tiny
white caracols.

Black Caracas

The children, seated,
are hearing a story.
The river was bringing us
wind crowns,
& a snake a big snake
from a very old tree trunk
watched the round clouds
in the sky.
My child, my chico,
where are you? I feel you
here in my heart
but not so. Way out there
you're waiting for me, till I pluck
your soul from the silence.

Big caracols
black caracols.

[EPITAPH FOR A BIRD]

[...........]

and its eyes as deep
as centuries, beside
the iridescence, pearl-like,
of its beak
Adiós green bird
You must already be in Limbo
Visit with my brother
Luisillo out there in the country
with his babes
Oh green bird adiós,
so big so small
You incredible chimera,
lemon bird narcissus!

Thanksgiving

Thank thee dear distant
God & Father mine
who gives me unimagined
lessons in poesis.

Oh holy holy holy
who does show the godly
hour of death,
unveiled, unto my soul!

Give me the dignity
this dear bird had, the rhythm
of its open wings
before the dark.

Oh holy holy holy
whom I ask this night to grant me
water for my eyes, & oh
thy shadow for my cry.

Memento

I have laid out the singer
on a great chrysanthemum
& I have writ his epitaph.

Memento.

Earth sleeps beneath
her windy veil,
her stormy seas
gone into calm.

Memento.

Now should the stars
raise questions,
you will know the answers
they cannot comprehend.

Memento.

You'll be laid out tonight
on a poet's bed.
What child ever dreamed
a dream inside a flower?

Memento.

And tonight I will send
as a guard for your body
the enormous butterfly
of my only kiss.

Memento!

WATER JETS

Interior

From my room I hear
the water jet.
A finger of grapevine
& a trace of sunlight
pointing to the place
where my heart is.

Through the August air
the clouds roll by, I
dream I'm not dreaming
inside the water jet.

Homeland

Water jets in dreams
sans water
& sans fountains!

Are detected from the corner
of the eye, & never face
to face.

Like all ideal
things, swaying
at the perfect boundaries
of Death.

Aside

Night's blood
flows through the arteries
of water jets.
Oh what a gorgeous
quaking!
I think of
open windows,
sans pianos
& sans maids.

*

[. . . . .]

Only right then it was!
The cloud of dust still
swaying, in the blue.
Only just now it was.
Two thousand centuries!
if I remember right.

Garden

There are four caballeros
with four swords made of water
& a very dark night.
The four swords are wounding
a world filled with roses
& will wound your hearts too.
Don't go down into that garden!

HERBALS

[1]

Book

The voyager in gardens
carries an herbal with him.
On his manual of odors,
whirls around.

At night onto its branches come
the souls of ancient birds.

They sing in that tight forest,
so needful of a fount of tears.

Like the noses of small children
pressed to a dark windowpane
are the flowers in this book of flowers
against the years' blank glass.

The voyager in gardens
opens his book, begins to cry,
& the errant colors
in his herbal fade & die.

[II]

The voyager through time
carries the herbal book of dreams.

I
Where is the herbal?

The Voyager
You have it in your hands.

I
I have ten fingers free.

The Voyager
Dreams dance in your hair.

I
And how many centuries have passed?

The Voyager
My herbal is just an hour old.

I
Am I heading for evening or dawn?

The Voyager
The past's an unlivable world.

I
Oh, garden of bitter fruit.

The Voyager
Worse yet the herbal of moon.

[III]

In great secret, a friend
shows me the herbal of noise.

(Psst... Keep quiet!
Night's hanging down from the sky.)

In the light across a lost harbor
all the centuries' echoes rise.

(Psst… keep quiet!
Night's being swung by the wind.)

Pssst… keep quiet!
Old furies coil around my hands.

IN THE FOREST
OF THE LUNAR GRAPEFRUITS
(A Static Poem)

Prologue

I am going on a long trip.

On a silver mirror I find, long before dawn, the satchel & the clothing I'll need for those exotic countries & theoretical gardens.

Poor & peaceful, I want to visit the static world, where all my possibilities live & all my lost landscapes. I want to get in there, cold & sharp, to find a garden of flowerless seeds & blind theories: in search of a love I never had but that once was mine.

Many's the long day that I searched—in every mirror in my house—for the road that leads to that marvelous garden. And at last—by pure chance!—I've found it.

I used many ploys. For a start I tried singing, keeping my voice big & tense in the air, but the mirrors stayed silent. I made complicated geometries with words & rhythms, I filled silvery eyes with my lament, I even placed a shade on the nightlight that illuminates the grotto in my head. But nothing helped.

One murky morning, after I had all but given up the idea of the trip & was feeling free of worries & invisible gardens, I went to comb my hair in front of a mirror, and without my asking it anything, its broad silver face filled up with a zigzag of nightingales singing, and in its mercurial depths the clear, precise key came to light—that key that I'm forbidden from revealing.

Now I'm setting out serenely on my voyage & truth to tell I'm washing my hands of it. I'll let you know what all I see there, just don't ask me to explain it.

I could have gone to the country of the dead, but I prefer going to the country of the unliving, which is not the same.

And truth to tell a *pure & intact soul* would not feel this kind of curiosity. I'm going at it free & easy. In the satchel I've got a good supply of glowworms.

Before taking off just now I felt a sharp pain in my heart. My family is sleeping & the whole house is in a state of absolute repose. The dawn reveals towers & one by one counts up the tree leaves. It slips a white mask on me & some kind of gloves [....]

Reflection

You who come and go,
run from river & from wind,
close your eyes &...
... & gather in your tears.

With soul tied on a string,
forget the question.
No need to wield interrogator's
sickle.

Question is the ivy
that covers & disjuncts us,

right before our eyes it spins
prisms & a crossroads.

Answer is the same as
question, but disguised.
Starts as spring of water,
comes back around as mirror.

[…]

The Three Disillusioning Witches
(*At the garden gate*)

1st Witch
Aiie for the toad flute
& aiie for the worm light!

2nd Witch
Aiie for the phosphorous sea
& aiie for the steel forests!

3rd Witch
Our enemy is the white
light with its seven colors.

1st Witch
My tears will spawn the black
rainbow of black light.

2nd Witch
Let things move back, move back
onto their primary planes.

3rd Witch
Kingdom of the seed
& the ecstatic dark.

2nd Witch
World without eyes, world
without labyrinths or reflections.

3rd Witch
Theories. Tall-rising towers
without foundations or stones.

1st Witch
Toad flute.
Worm light.

All Three
Each thing in its circle.
Everything unknown.
Wind that will not answer
questions from the tree.

3rd Witch
Kingdom of the seed
& the ecstatic dark.

2nd Witch
Ah poor mistaken flower
on its unknowing stem!

1st Witch
Sisters, blind the pupils in
the white dragon's seven eyes.

All Three
Each thing in its circle.
Everything unknown.
We are worn out, cockeyed,
gone to the same old place.

★

[. . . . .]

Behind the door comes the laughter
of two skulls with wings.

Who goes there?

I'm off to the forest no one can enter—
the forest of grapefruits, of moons.

Jam it down—spit it up—that mouthful
of Adam's.
        The door's lost its leaves.

Three huge smiles, with no teeth,
devour my cool little smile.

[...]

Situation

The first windsnake twists
among the sapless poplars.

I have a huge beard,
just like old man river.

I recall the old crowds,
blind nights, sleepwalking birds.
My century's a graywater river
& my catboat is under lead sails.

Such ennui of skies on my eyeballs!
A spasm—perennial dawn—
imprisons my aged flesh
in its stiff, hectic branches.

Clang-clang
(The Earth was heading off, paved over with domes
under the atmosphere's eggshell blue.)

Who goes there?

(Between milklight & moonlight
I arrive at the tower where the others await me.)

Tower

He was there
with his crown of
loud heehaws.
Big yellow beard.

He
I was waiting for you.

I
The skeleton key to the Dream
opened your house for me.

What now is alive
never lived
nor will live. My eyes,
filled with hoarfrost, mimic
white motionless forests.

He
Inside each star
's a gold worm.
Dragon hides smile of a child
'neath its wing.

I
Ah you beggar! Ah you bugger!
I've got nothing to offer you.
Not a smile, not a worm!

He
Mister, you're a hundred years old.

I
Not a hundred, no, on my shoulders
each year's a long
sword of quivering light.

He
How did you get past the river
& past the water butterflies?

I
With the key to the Dream—
in spite of your meddling.

He

                              Give me
your lips.

I
        No. Can't be done!
Not my garden of words.

He
Are you trembling? Look at your world.

The Bells (in the distance)
        Cling clang
        Cling clang

Ah, that Christmas in your house!
The moon spawning turquoises
to a tinpan rhythm.
That one was born out of mud.
Ah, that Christmas in your house!
We bells saw you
—heartless & faceless—
making bridges and horsewhips
turn gray like your soul.

      Cling clang
      Cling clang

Adiós, adiós, and Remember,
thou poor misguided light!
Gigantic spikenards of darkness
encircle thy ancient house.

      Cling clang
      Cling clang

He
Soul crippled but crystal clear,
come look at the garden!

The ancient full-moons
—like immense crystal discs—
sparkle propped in the foliage.

The Bells in the Tower (alone)
    Ah! Ah!
When will we sleep?
The shadow weighs heavy, over
our lidless eyes.
When will we sleep?
Only cut off our flowers,
or get us a diving mask.
    Ah! Ah!

IN THE GARDEN
OF THE LUNAR GRAPEFRUITS

Prologue

> *So like the shadow our life doth slip away*
> *that never doth return nor us restore.*
> —PERO LÓPEZ DE AYALA *(Consejos morales)*

I have taken leave of the friends I love the most &
have set out on a short dramatic journey. On a silver
mirror I find, long before dawn, the satchel with
the clothing I'll need for the exotic country to
which I'm heading.

The tight, cold scent of sunrise beats weirdly on
the huge escarpment we call night.

On the sky's stretched page a cloud's initial letter
trembles, & below my balcony a nightingale & frog
raise up a sleepy cross of sound.

I—tranquil, melancholy man—make my final
preparations, impeded by those subtlest feelings
aroused in me by wings & by concentric circles. On
the white wall in my room, stiff & rigid like a snake
in a museum, hangs the noble sword my grand-

father carried in the war against Don Carlos the Pretender.

With reverence I take the sword down, coated with yellow rust like a white poplar, & I gird it on me while remembering that I'll have to go through an awful invisible fight before I enter the garden. An ecstatic & ferocious fight against my secular enemy, the giant dragon Common Sense.

A sharp & elegiac feeling for things that haven't been—good & evil, large & small—invades those landscapes in back of my eyes that my ultraviolet glasses have all but occulted. A bitter feeling that makes me travel toward this garden that shimmers on its skyhigh prairie.

The eyes of all creatures pound like phosphorescent points against the wall of the future... what was past stays filled with yellowing underbrush, orchards without any fruit, waterless rivers. No man ever fell backwards into death. But I, absorbed for now by this abandoned & infinite landscape, catch a glimpse of life's unpublished blueprints—multiplied, superposed, like buckets in an endless waterwheel.

Before taking off just now I felt a sharp pain in my heart. My family is sleeping & the whole house is in a state of absolute repose. The dawn reveals towers & one by one counts up the tree leaves. It slips a costume on me: crackling, made of spangled lace.

Must be something I've forgotten… can't be any doubt about it, so much time spent getting ready &… lord, what is it that escapes me? Ah, a piece of wood…a piece of good old cherry wood… rose-colored, tight-grained.

I believe in being well-groomed when I travel…. From a jar of flowers on my nightstand, I pick out a huge pale rose & pin it to my left lapel. It has a fierce but hieratic face.

And so the time has come.

(With the scatterbrained sound of the bells' tongues come the cockadoodledoos of the roosters.)

Portico

    CHILD: *I am going in search of*
    the gryphon-bird's wings.
    DWARF: *My child, there is no way*
    I can help you in this matter.
      —*Old folk tale*

    Clang clang

The air, having been killed,
lay motionless & shriveled.

The pinetrees, living, lay on the earth.
Their shadows uprisen, trembling!

    I—You—He
    (on a single plane)

    Clang clang

[…]

Perspective

From behind my eyes
hermetic song breaks open—
song of the seedling that
did not ever flower.

Each one dreams about an
unreal, quirky end.
(The wheat dreams it's got
enormous yellow flowers.)

All of them dreaming strange
adventures in the shade.
Fruits hanging out of reach
& domesticated winds.

None of them know each other,
blind & gone astray,
their perfumes paining them
but cloistered now forever.

Each seed thinks up
a genealogical tree—
covers the whole sky
with its stalks & roots.

The air's smeared over with
improbable vegetations.
Black & heavy branches.
Cinder-colored roses.

The moon nearly smothered
with flowers & with branches
fights them off with moonbeams
like an octopus in silver.

From behind my eyes
hermetic song breaks open—
song of the seedlings that
did not ever flower.

The Garden

was never born, never,
but could burst into life.

Every moment it's
deepened, restored.

Every moment it opens new
unheard-of pathways.

Over here! over there!
See my multiple bodies

passing through pueblos
or asleep in the ocean.

Everything open! Locks
to fit every key.
But the sun & moon
lose & delude us
& under our feet
the highways are tangled.

Here I'll mull over all
I once could have been.
God or beggar,
water or old marguerite.

My multiple paths
barely stained
now form this enormous rose
encircling my body.

Like an impossible map
the garden of the possible
every moment is
deepened, restored.

Was never born, never,
but could burst into life.

Pergola

A static jet of water,
over which
a large dead bird's
asleep.

Two lovers kissing
in among
Dream's icy
crystals.

"The ring, hand me the ring."
"I can't see where my fingers are."

"Why don't you hold me?"

    "No, my arms
are bent & freezing
on the bed."

Dragging along, between
the leaves,
a trace of the old moon.

Avenue

Pallid white theories
with blindfolded eyes
would dance through the forest.

Sluggish like swans
& bitter like oleander.

They passed by, unseen
by a man's eyes,
as at nightfall the rivers
pass by, unreported.
As in the silence, a new-
fangled murmuring.

One of them inside her gown
has a gray heavy look
as of somebody dying.
                              Others
shake outsized branches of
disjuncted words.

They don't live, are alive,
pass through the ecstatic forest.
A swarm of sleepwalking women!
(Sluggish like swans
& bitter like oleander.)

Women leaving an odor behind them,
mental, stripped of appearances,
the air as indifferent as ever,
like a white camellia, a hundred blossoms.

Song of the Motionless Gardener

What you wouldn't have suspected
lives & trembles in the air.

Those treasures of the day
you keep just out of reach.

These come & go in truckloads
but no one stops to see them.

Banged up they come but virgin,
& gone back to seed they leave.

Things speak to you but no one
bothers to stop & listen.

The world's a waterspout of
objects, various & steady.

Those treasures of the day
you keep just out of reach.

The hot rush of your blood
drowning the virgin silence.

But the two good eyes you have
would draw you to the source.

Those treasures of the day
you keep just out of reach.

What you wouldn't have suspected
lives & trembles in the air.

The garden joined together
by its putrefying perfumes.

Every leaf inside it dreaming
a different kind of dream.

Floating Bridges

Oh what a crush of people
invisible   reborn
make their way into this garden
for their eternal rest!

Every step we take on earth
brings us to a new world.
Every foot supported
on a floating bridge.

And I know that there is no
straight road in this world—
only a giant labyrinth
of intersecting crossroads.

And steadily our feet
keep walking & creating
—like enormous fans—
these roads in embryo.

Oh garden of white
theories! garden
of all I am not, all
I could & should have been!

White Satyr

Atop deathless narcissuses
the white satyr slept.

Huge horns made of crystal
virginized his deep brows.

The sun, a tamed dragon,
licked his ladylike hands.

On the river of love
dead nymphs drifted by.

The satyr's heart in the wind
dried out from old storms.

The syringe on the ground
was a fountain,

it had seven blue tubes
cut in glass.

Engravings of the Garden

[1]

Those antique virgins
still unloved,
walk with their loverboys
through silent leaves.

The boys, how eyeless
& how wordless they,
who cover themselves with smiles
like curlicues of feathers.

Strutting beneath the gray
& frosty tulips—
a white delirium
of cloistered lights.

Blind crowd—the perfumes
drifting past—
their feet propped up on
uncut flowers.

Oh deep & crooked light
from oranges gone numb!
And loverboys who stumble
over their broken swords.

[II]

Widow of the moon—
who could forget her?
Dreaming that the earth
be crystal,

she, furious & pale,
would rock the sea to sleep,
comb out her tresses
with coral, like a cry.

Hairs spun of glass—
who could forget them?
At her breast a hundred
lips, a single fountain.

Halberds from giant
jets spurt up,
keep guard of her by silent
waves, by dunes.

But moon, the moon,
when will the moon come back?
A curtain made of wind
that trembles on and on.

Widow of the moon—
who could forget her?
Dreaming that the earth
be crystal.

Like thee, good count Arnaldo,
who would forget thee too?
Thee, dreaming a whole earth
in crystal.

[. . . . .]

I
What do you want from me, Dream,
that you won't let me be?

Dream
A dozen gold swans
& a dozen black moons.

I
I want clear days & nights
& no secrets.

Dream
[. . . . .]

Moonbow

A bow of black moons
over the motionless sea.

My unborn children
track me down.

"Father, don't run from us, wait,
the youngest of us is dying."

They hang themselves from my eyes.
The cock starts to crow.

The sea, turned to stone, is laughing
a last laugh made of waves.

"Father, don't run from us!"...
                              And my screams

turning to spikenards.

*

Tall towers.
Wide waters.

Fairy
Take this wedding ring
that your grandfathers wore.
A hundred hands under the earth
will be grieving its absence.
I
I'm going to feel in my hands
a huge flower of fingers
& the symbol of that ring.
Oh ring I do not want!

Tall towers.
Wide waters.

Little Song of the Unborn Child

On a flower of dark sobs
& waters you left me.

The lament that I learned
will be a shriveled old man
dragging sighs & tears
behind it like a tail.

If I have no arms,
how will I force daylight's door?
Those oars served another
child on his boat.

I was sleeping in peace.
Who ripped into my dream?
My mother has long had
a head of white hair.

On a flower of dark sobs
& waters you left me.

Song of the Seven-Hearted Boy

Seven hearts
are the hearts that I have.
But mine is not there among them.

In the high mountains, mother,
where I sometimes ran into the wind,
seven girls with long hands
carried me around in their mirrors.

I have sung my way through this world
with my mouth with its seven petals.
My crimson-colored galleys
have cast off without rigging or oars.

I have lived my life in landscapes
that other men have owned.
And the secrets I wore at my throat,
unbeknownst to me, had come open.

In the high mountains, mother,
where my heart rises over its echoes
in the memory book of a star,
I sometimes ran into the wind.

Seven hearts
are the hearts that I have.
But mine is not there among them.

White Smell

Oh what cold perfumes
what hyacinths!

What maiden who comes
through white cypresses.
Carries her two severed breasts
on a platter of gold.

(Two highways.
Her very long train
& the milky way.)

Mother of stillborns
who shudders
with the frenzy of light-worms.

Oh what cold perfumes
what hyacinths!

Encounter

> Sun flower.
> River flower.

I
Was it you? Your breast so blazing
with light I lost sight of you.

She
And my dress with its ribbons—
how many times did it brush you?

I
In your throat I can hear, unopened,
my children's white voices.

She
Your children afloat in my eyes
are yellow like diamonds.

I
Was it you? Where were you dragging
your unending tresses, my love?

She
On the moon—are you laughing?
then circling Narcissus' flower.

I
In my breast a snake that won't sleep
but quakes with old kisses.

She
The moments fell open & fastened
their roots on my sighs.

I
Joined by one breeze
face to face, we were strangers!

She
The branches are burgeoning,
                              go from me!
Neither of us has been born.

        Sun flower.
        River flower.

Dune

Atop that vast dune
—most ancient light—
I find myself lost
with no sky, no road.

The North near to death
had switched off its stars.
The skies were shipwrecked,
slowly rising & falling.

Through a sea made of light
I go where? I seek whom?
A reflection that cries here
—of moons hidden by veils.

May the cool piece of tight-grained
wood in my hand
take me back to my balcony—
my still living birds.

Then the garden will follow,
will be moving its borders
on the coarse-grained shoulders
of a silence run aground.

Wake Up/Ring Out
(Outside the garden)

Sun with his hundred horns
lifts the downed sky.

Same motion repeated by
the bulls on the prairie.

Spectacular rain of stones
around the old bell towers

arouses the wind, drives
its vast herd down the road.

In the river the wars
of the fish are beginning.

My soul, boy & girl,
be silent, *silent!*

APPENDIX
TO SUITES

Train Ride

Sundown's mouth bites
mountain's chalk.
A girl star
's run away in
her blue sky.

Old Melancholy

Landscape's got
a century of cobwebs.
Storage bin for sunsets
& for nights.

A Salutation

From my shadow
among lilies, filled up
with the melancholy
of the good man

who saw the bleeding of
a newborn love (white,
wingless swan) by inches
& who wants to clip the lonely
spectral rose the dawn
pretends to be,
I set my lyric bell to ringing
on this lovely morning
with its dreamy
wind…

How terminal my sadness,
daubs itself with rouge & learns
your wondrous love.
This sadness that invades
my sleepy heart
alive by chance
gray   gray.

Coaldust in my eyes
& Satan's fingernails
scratching my breast.
Satan,

my old boyhood friend.
The train, a mole,
gnaws at the wind's roots
& goes on.

Distances of bells.
Plows dormant.
Lyric furrows.

Evening nodding out
the domino of colors
faded.

A guitar that says
"My wood is cypress."
Somnolence in G sharp for bassoon & strings.
Vibrations.
And at the railroad crossings
an arm gives you the shaft.

Afterwards
(On the undecidable prairie)

I've pulled up to the doorway
of *Then.*
Hand me down my guitar!
The whole world is white.
Hand me down my guitar!
I'm off to count pines
on that mountain,
sands
in the saltsavored sea.
Left the vale of tears
back in the wind
gone to have a sweet time
find a beach for my soul.

(I've got goldrimmed glasses
& an orangecolored tux)

Open Door

Open doors
all give on a chasm
much deeper
the older the house is.

But a door
is no door
until a dead man
comes through it,
looks around mournfully,
crucified
on the bloodspattered morning.

What sweat
to get past the thresholds
of all these damned doors!
Inside we see a blind
lamp,
see a girl hide in fear of
the weather.

The door is always the key
to the story.
Rose with two petals
blown open & shut
by the wind.

From Out Here

Tell my friends
that I'm dead.

The water sings endlessly
down where the forest is rumbling.

Tell my friends
that I'm dead.
(The poplars are waving
gauzes of sound!)

Tell them I'm out here
with my eyes wide open,

my face covered up
by this deathless bandana,
the sky.

      Ah!

Gone off without bread
to my own shining star.

Evening

It's now the hour
for being sincere
the hour for groans
without letup
the last hour before
the big silence.
Step out of your clothes
flesh & bones
puke up
your sick hearts.
With groans & greetings amigos!

Watch out for those winds
stuffed with seeds
& unpublished landscapes
Blossom, & tear out
your blossoms anew
unspeakably dressed
heart   flesh   bones.
With groans & greetings amigos!
In front of the sea of the winds
be always alive, be
eternally dying.

[I]

The City

To Guillermo de Torre

The tower says: "up to here"
& the cypress: "me up to there."

Men & women are making
a babel out of words.

Raging across the rooftops
frantic zigzags, ellipses.

The city covers its forehead
with smoky feathers & screams.

(They all look for what
they can't find.)

And the grass grows in front of
the portico of Up There.

[II]

The Reaction

My heart go away
with your know-it-all turtles
my heart go & find
a Sahara of light!

My heart go away
with your know-it-all turtles
a spiral for your body
& wings for your soul.

Decked out like the pope
with their pluvial capes
turtles can teach us
the uselessness of feet.

They can cut through the flimflam
of celestial horizons
& dedicate their lives
to studying a star
a star with which
to impregnate their shells.

My heart go away
with your know-it-all turtles.
A spiral for your body
& wings for your soul
you aren't going to need them
when you feel the ground shake!

My heart put to rest
your old hunger for limits.

GREEN INTEGER
Pataphysics and Pedantry

Edited by Per Bregne
Douglas Messerli, *Publisher*

Essays, Manifestos, Statements, Speeches, Maxims,
Epistles, Diaristic Notes, Narratives, Natural Histories,
Poems, Plays, Performances, Ramblings, Revelations
and all such ephemera as may appear necessary
to bring society into a slight tremolo of confusion
and fright at least.

*

Green Integer Books

*3 Masterpieces of Cuban Drama: Plays by
Juilo Matas, Carlos Felipe, and Vigilio Piñera*
Translated and Edited with an Introduction by
Luis F. González-Cruz and Ann Waggoner Aken [2000]
Antilyrik and Other Poems Vítězslav Nezval [2001]
Rectification of Eros Sam Eisenstein [2000]
Drifting Dominic Cheung [2000]
Gold Fools Gilbert Sorrentino [2001]
Erotic Recipes Jiao Tung [2001]
The Mysterious Hualien Chen I-chih [2001]

Green Integer EL-E-PHANT books:

The PIP Anthology of World Poetry of the 20th Century, Volume 1
Douglas Messerli, editor [2000]
The PIP Anthology of World Poetry of the 20th Century, Volume 2
Douglas Messerli, editor [2001]
readiness / enough / depends / on Larry Eigner [2000]
Two Fields that Face and Mirror Each Other Martin Nakell [2001]

BOOKS FORTHCOMING FROM GREEN INTEGER

Islands and Other Essays Jean Grenier
The Doll and *The Doll at Play* Hans Bellmer
[with poetry by Paul Éluard]
American Notes Charles Dickens
Prefaces and Essays on Poetry
William Wordsworth
Confessions of an English Opium-Eater
Thomas De Quincey
The Renaissance Walter Pater
Captain Nemo's Library Per Olav Enquist
Partial Portraits Henry James